JOY TO THE WORLD

JOY TO THE WORLD

24 meditations on the best news ever
and how to live it every day

Chris Stefanick

JAMESON PRESS

2016

Joy to the World

Published by Jameson Press

2 3 4 5 6 7 8 9 10

Printed in the United States of America.
ISBN 978-0-9981688-0-7

Cover Design: Cassie Pease
Interior Design: Sherry Russell, Russell Graphic Design

Real Life Catholic
www.RealLifeCatholic.com
Email: info@RealLifeCatholic.com

For more information on this title and other books and CDs available through Real Life Catholic, please visit RealLifeCatholic.com.

Table of Contents

3/15/?? Habits of Holy People

① Love Yourself ~ ~~words~~ Speak the word of
God to yourself
I am blessed, beautiful, chosen & a
daughter of God.

② Love Yourself ~ Actions :

② Pray : Enter in the presence of Love
Conversation - Speak + Listen
to His Word

③ Share the Faith
through the witness of my life
(perfect vs authentic)

④ Friendship : "How are you?"

⑤ Reboot   God gives me the ability to
start over everyday

covenant eyes.
com

Jesus died to
give me the
chance to reboot
(& be forgiven)

Part I

THE BEST NEWS EVER

Joy to the world!

There is no better news:

Your deepest hopes aren't answered by the void,

but by the Word.

The story of human existence is a love story.

Death doesn't get the final word.

Love wins.

You were created for glory.

That "something more"

you're looking for is within reach

and it's free for the taking.

Nothing comes close.

There is no message taught by any philosopher,

no dream dreamt by any child

no book penned by any author

no pleasure offered by the world,

that's as stunningly beautiful

or able to fill our souls with

purpose and peace.

And the best part is:

It's not for someone else.

It's for you.

Now.

The first Christians summed up the central message of Christianity with a funny word: *Kerygma.* It's a word taken up from the ancient Greek world. It means "announcement." It's what a *keryx* (a herald) did.

Before print, the way you got news out to the world was to entrust it to a herald, who spread it from town to town. He'd show up in the city center, unroll a scroll on behalf of a king, and shout, "Hear ye! Hear ye!"

The reason the first Christians used that word to describe the core message of the Gospel is simple: They didn't see Christianity as an intellectual endeavor reserved for the greatest minds. They didn't see Christianity as a secret spiritual path only for the most enlightened souls. They didn't see Christianity as a moral code for the perfect. They saw Christianity as the best news ever.

"I bring you good news of great joy" (Luke 2:10).

What is that news? God is with us!

The most beautiful sound I've ever heard (and I've been blessed to hear it six times) is the first sound of my baby's voice piercing the air with a cry that announces, "I am here! This passing universe (and your life, Dad) will never be the same!"

When Jesus was born he made that same cry. It's also the first announcement of his public ministry: "The kingdom is at hand." In other words, "I am here. Nothing will ever be the same. I make all things new."

The announcement of God's presence among us is news so big that the whole story of the universe fits under the headline. News so powerful it rewrites the story of our lives. News so personal it reads like a love letter.

Every Christmas we're invited to remember what that news is, and what it has to do with our own quest for *something more . . .*

Long lay the world, in sin and error pining

Like the deer that longs for running streams, so my soul longs for God. —Psalm 42:1

Jesus' first interaction with mankind in the Gospel of John is kind of awkward. He noticed two men following him and stopped, looked straight at them, and said, "What are you looking for?"

I think he wanted them to stop and ask themselves that question before taking another step. He wants us to ask it of ourselves, too—because that question is the start of the spiritual journey. More than almost anything else, what we desire shapes who we become. When we desire the wrong things (sin and error), we end up empty—pining—even after we've had our fill. We need to shape our desires rather than being shaped by them.

Our longing for "something more" than this world can offer has led man to think of God since the dawn of time.

If we're losing touch with God today it's probably because we've lost touch with ourselves. We've lost touch with our longing. We ignore our deepest longings and ideals when they're drowned out by the "noise" of passing news and countless to-dos. Or worse, we tend to suppress our highest hopes when life leaves us hurt and disappointed. Or if we've had the courage to encounter our fundamental longing, we seek to satisfy it quickly with lesser pleasures.

I want you to give yourself permission to ask the dangerous, uncomfortable questions: "What do I want out of life? What am I looking for? *Really?*"

If you dig deep, you'll find that, beneath every answer from "a happy marriage" to "a big fat paycheck" to "fame and fortune" (all of which you may or may not get) is a deeper longing. We want *more.* We want happiness. We want joy. We want peace. We want LOVE. But we don't just want a little of those things. We want an infinite supply—more of it than this whole world could possibly give! We want GLORY!

. . . Let yourself feel that longing . . .

That would be cruel advice if that longing had no answer! Thankfully it does have an answer. The one who

12

asked the question "What are you looking for?" *is* the an-swer. He just wants you to find that out for yourself and to begin directing that longing to him. That's what the spiritual journey is all about.

I wonder as I wander out under the sky

Foolish by nature were all who were in ignorance of God and who . . . from studying the works did not discern the artisan. —Wisdom 13

One atheist was trying to debate me online (this happens often): "Chris, you believing in God is like as a kid looking under his Christmas tree, seeing presents and saying, 'Oh look, presents, there must be a Santa!'"

"Really?" I wrote back. "Because you not believing in God is like a kid coming down on Christmas morning, seeing presents under the tree and saying, 'Oh look, presents, they must have exploded themselves here!'" A child might get the identity of the gift giver wrong, but when he sees presents he knows they didn't put themselves there. Space and time did not put themselves here.

An atheist Russian cosmonaut is credited with looking around in space and saying, "Well, I'm here, and I don't see God anywhere." That would be like Frodo reaching the summit of Mount Doom and saying, "There's no evidence of J.R.R. Tolkien anywhere!" God isn't something *in* space and time that we can study under a microscope. Space and time are in him. "In him we live, we move and have our being."

I think we're the first generation to have such a growing number of people ask, "If there's really a God, why doesn't he reveal himself?" I can almost hear him answer, "Did you not notice *everything*?!?"

And maybe the sad answer is that we don't. We forget to contemplate the world all around us just like we forget to listen to the longing in our own hearts, or maybe both would call us back to God.

St. Augustine wrote that we should "Question the beauty of the earth, question the beauty of the sea, question the beauty of the air . . . question the beauty of the sky . . . the sun making the day glorious with its bright beams . . . the moon tempering the darkness . . . with its shining rays, question the animals that move in the waters, that amble about on dry land . . . question all these things. They all answer you, 'Here we are, look; we're beautiful.' Their beauty is their confession. Who made these beautiful changeable things, if not one who is beautiful and unchangeable?"

All creation shouts to us that there's a God! And just as a painting gives an insight into the heart of an artist, creation tells us that God is beautiful. But if we don't take the time to notice—to question the beauty all around—we won't hear that.

In the words of Martin Luther, "God writes the Gospel not in the bible alone, but also on trees, and in the flowers and clouds and stars."

God wrote two books: Scripture and Creation. We should spend time reading both. I know you're busy. Everyone is. But STOP for a minute and smell the roses today! (I mean that literally.) Take a deep breath. Get your head out of your phone and look around. You might hear creation shouting to *you*.

And Heaven and nature sing

God is love. —1 John 4:8

We love love stories. It's as if we're made for them.

The first time I saw my wife I was at Mass scoping the church for a girlfriend. (Don't judge me.) I noticed her and was blown away. "She's out of my league," I thought. Thankfully, she didn't agree. On our second date I played "Annie's Song" to her on my guitar.

"Stop!" she said.

"Why?"

"I'll tell you later."

Later she told me that ever since she was a little girl she thought the first guy that played that to her would be the guy she married. Alleluia!

And so began a love story. But that particular story, like all our love stories, is only one part of a greater narrative that we're each caught up in. All of life is a love story. The author is God.

The love story starts before space and time. Reason shows us *that* there is a God. Faith shows us *who* God is. We know the power that was capable of starting all of this because he revealed himself to us: Love. "God is love." And love is not a vague "force." Love is personal.

I can almost see him smile in that quiet "moment" before space and time began. In the words of St. John Paul II, "The joy of living reflects the original joy that God felt in creating us." And so, Love sent *being* exploding like a billion ribbons of light and heat into the void at incomprehensible speed.

And he did it with you in mind. He created space and time so he could put you in it. It's the stage for *the* love story, and the place where God wanted to meet you, surrounded by the most vast and beautiful backdrop, from nearby flowers to far-flung galaxies, and filled with experiences of life and love and joy and sorrow, all of it, pages in a story leading us to the love that made us for himself.

When we begin to see life in the pure light of that love, when we begin to reexamine old memories and open ourselves to new experiences as pages in the most epic love story ever told, we begin to see that life is beautiful.

Hail, hail, the Word made flesh, the babe, the son of Mary

And the Word became flesh and made his dwelling among us. —John 1:14

That a baby who could fit in your arms is the maker of space and time is the most audacious claim made by any faith ever. So why do we believe it? Because Jesus taught us who he was, and he verified his claims with the most amazing miracle of all time.

Jesus wasn't put to death for being a political activist. He was put to death for "blasphemy." By his words and actions, he taught people that he was divine. From the very first days of the Church, the early Christians worshipped him as God.

How do we know those early Christians were right?

Because Jesus rose from the dead.

Harvard law professor Dr. Simon Greenleaf set out to debunk Christianity. He thought "everything these people believe rests on their claim that Jesus rose from the dead, but that wouldn't even hold up in court!"

But the more he researched, the more he ran into a problem. Jesus' Resurrection *would* hold up in court. If someone is tried for a crime, if there are eyewitnesses, he's going to jail. And if every eyewitness is willing to die rather than retract his claim, the person on trial has no hope of staying out of jail! That's what we have with the Resurrection. Jesus' first followers didn't die for a vague "belief." They died gruesome deaths, from an upside-down crucifixion to being flayed alive, because they had seen Jesus risen from the dead. They wouldn't have done that for a lie.

Dr. Greenleaf became a Christian.

The love story that is Christianity is the best news imaginable, and the best part about it is that it's real. *Really* real. There is a God. And although the story of faith is usually the story of man seeking God, what happened in Bethlehem two thousand years ago is God looking for us. Looking for you.

Little baby . . .
I am a poor boy too

You will find a baby wrapped in swaddling clothes. —Luke 2:12

It's a bit hard to believe. Shouldn't the divine be something more . . . well . . . profound? Shouldn't *truly* spiritual things be sublime? Dizzying to the intellect? Blinding to the eye? Ever beyond our grasp?

Some people presume that Christianity is shallow because we "put God in a box," so to speak. They reject Jesus because he's too ordinary. Too small. Too definable. "Cute," almost. As if a God who is vague and hidden behind the clouds is more "profound" than the God who loved us enough to reveal himself to us! (Or maybe some people prefer a vague God because that doesn't demand much from us?)

But nothing is more profound than love.

My friend Ryan had been exploring Christianity over many late nights at the pub with my (then) girlfriend (now wife) and me for almost two years. He'd grown up a "devout" agnostic. In a beautiful "aha!" moment, he summed up the Faith better than I ever could for him: "If there's a God, he's Catholic." He said, "I just can't imagine him being anything less than the love that you guys say he is." Ryan was baptized the following Easter.

And if God is love, the absurdity of the manger is the only thing that makes any sense.

Sure, he could have stayed hidden behind the veil of space and time—an undefinable force—but love wanted intimacy with us. He could have come riding on the clouds, lightning bolts and all, one of the Zeus-like gods we'd always dreamt up. But he didn't come to wow us. He came to woo us. He didn't come looking for our submission. He came looking for our hearts. He came to us as a servant. He comes as plain as bread.

We didn't put God "in a box." He put himself in one for us.

In Bethlehem there is a massive basilica. The door to enter it is very small. You have to bow down to get in. It's called "the door of humility." Love humbled himself to meet us where we were at. We need humility to see it. He became poor for us. We need to become poor in spirit to receive it.

Love has driven God to become so plain. So approachable. So mind-blowingly ordinary that it's hard to accept. And I can't imagine God being anything less vast, profound, beautiful, and radical than that. Can you?

That's the kind of "radical" he's inviting us to be for one another.

Fall on your knees. Oh hear the angel voices!

… and we saw his glory, the glory as of the Father's only Son, full of grace and truth. —John 1:14

A lot of people think faith is boring. Maybe we're boring. In the words of G.K. Chesterton, "The world is dry not for lack of wonders but for lack of wonder."

We tend to get bored of the most amazing things. We lose our wonder. When I first got a cell phone I was in awe of the fact that my voice went into space from that little device and back down into whatever number I had dialed. Now, thanks to my smartphone, I have access to all the information in history in the palm of my hand and when it takes too long to access all that information I get angry. I've gone from total amazement to completely taking it for granted.

We do that with each other all the time. The people closest to us are usually the first we take for granted. Kids take their parents for granted. (Thank your parent for getting to exist?) Spouses may have been in awe of one another while they were dating. A few years after their wedding day and if they aren't careful the daily grind can erode all gratitude for one another.

We do this with Jesus, too. He saw it coming. "No prophet is honored in his home town." Today, Jesus' "home town" is everywhere you can find a Church.

Where's our wonder?

Jesus is anything but dull. He walked on water, appeared before his apostles in dazzling light, and could make dead people rise by simply saying, "Get up." Beneath the rib cage of this ordinary baby in a manger beats the heart of God.

We might stop for a minute, contemplate, and cultivate some amazement about that, and while we're at it, it's a good time to start appreciating one another more, too.

Born that man no more may die

He himself bore our sins in his body on the cross. —1 Peter 2:24

I arrived at a car accident the other day before the police did. As I walked past the wreckage I fully expected to see someone dead, or nearly. The side of the car was split open, its parts spilled everywhere, the axle exposed and wheel far from the wreck, a pool of gasoline forming on the ground.

Thankfully (and maybe miraculously) the passengers looked like they'd be okay. The driver, a young man, was sitting beside the car bleeding heavily from the head, but he was stable. The girl who had been in the passenger's seat was okay, too, aside from minor lacerations and obvious shock.

Witnesses said he had been going 80 in a 45, and had almost killed someone in the oncoming lane before he swerved into a wall.

As cops, ambulances, and firemen arrived at the scene, I wondered what caused such recklessness? That kind of driving is usually an expression of something *wrong* in the heart.

Was he driving like a maniac to impress a girl? Was he in a fight with her? I wondered if he was willing to risk his life that day because he places a cheap price tag on his own life. Maybe because he has deep-seated anger. Maybe he's angry at his dad. Maybe he's angry at his dad because his dad was distant, perhaps because his grandpa was abusive to his dad, perhaps because his great-grandpa was an alcoholic, and maybe that's because . . .

And it struck me: the generational impact of sin, the web of pain we all weave through our self-centeredness, is staggering. Maybe in two hundred years some young man will end up swerving into oncoming traffic because I yell at my kids too much. No sin is committed in isolation. And anyone who flaunts the fact that they have "no regrets" is either ignorant of their connectedness with humanity or doesn't care if they hurt others.

So how do we look straight on at the weight of sin, humanity's sin and our own, and not crumble?

When Jesus was crucified we saw all that is worst about the human condition converging on one man. Political factions, shirking of responsibility, good ol'-fashioned bloodlust, manipulation in the name of religion.

"Yet in thy dark streets shineth the everlasting light."

Look closer. Look into the center of the wreckage. In the midst of the dust and the blood there are open arms. The tenderness of Bethlehem completed in the self-giving love of the cross. The God who came to meet us in our brokenness and forgive us. The antidote for sin: Mercy. And more, we see the example for how we're to embrace the brokenness in others, and in ourselves.

Nails, spear shall pierce him through

God proves his love for us in this: While we were still sinners Christ died for us. —Romans 5:8

I had the worst twenty minutes of my life when we were camping and I lost my son Joey. He was four.

He had wandered into the woods, gotten disoriented, and sat down amidst the trees. My whole family was screaming his name but he was too scared to respond. Too scared to move.

I ran to the pond near our camp. I thought he must have drowned. I had no idea where else he could have been. So I was knee deep in the water, and as I looked for his body, a prayer exploded from my heart. It wasn't premeditated. It just came out of who I am as a dad—which is a little echo of who God is as my father.

"God, you've done so much good for me. You've given me a great life. You've given me so many blessings. Take it all back. And give me my son."

Thankfully we found Joey and God didn't take me up on my prayer.

But in that moment, he gave me the smallest glimpse of his love for you, and me.

In the scales of a father's love, one child outweighs everything.

And when we wandered from our created purpose into the forest of sin, God didn't look down from heaven and say, "I knew you'd do that. Go ahead. Enjoy being lost."

Instead, he reached out to mankind through Abraham, Isaac, Moses, and the prophets, with you in mind. And then "in the fullness of time God sent forth his Son, born of woman" (Gal. 4:4). That child was born for one primary purpose: To die. For you. Nails and a spear pierced him through. He is the love of God shouting to a fallen humanity, "Take everything. Take my life. I just want my son. I just want my daughter to come home."

All we need to do to begin following him is to agree to receive that love.

His law is love and His gospel is peace

He loved us first. —1 John 4:19

When we lose the context of love in a marriage, all we're left with is a bad idea.

- You have to give up all your closet space.
- You never keep your money for yourself ever again.
- You need to report your whereabouts to someone else at all times.

No, thanks.

But if you step back and see the big picture: that you get to give your life to a beautiful woman who gives hers in exchange, suddenly it's all worth it!

That's why it's so critical that married couples regularly step away from all the business, have a date night, and remember why they're doing all this!

The same is true with faith. It's a love story. When we forget that, it just looks like a bad idea. "We, the women and men of the Church, we are in the middle of a love story . . . And if we do not understand this, we have understood nothing of what the Church is" (Pope Francis), and Christianity "becomes a mere set of principles which are increasingly difficult to understand, and rules which are increasingly hard to accept" (St. John Paul II).

The world *has* forgotten. Sometimes we forget. And so the Faith looks like a bunch of rules, regulations, sacrifices, and doctrines that have nothing to do with *real life*. That's why the average person seeking "enlightenment" today wouldn't put the Church in the top ten places they'd go to find it. And often they don't only think the Church is irrelevant, they think it's ugly. And tragically, not just faith, but all of life starts to look ugly as a result.

A study was done in Great Britain that showed up to 22 percent of teenage girls had seriously considered suicide. Sometimes that's the result of a tragedy or a chemical imbalance. (If you're depressed, please talk to someone!) But a number that high isn't all chemical imbalances. It seems we've forgotten our story.

You're in the midst of an epic saga that started before time began. *You* are the object of a love that's more vast than the universe, mightier than the sea, as tender as a newborn infant. That love is inviting you to live and love as radically as he did, under the cloak of an "ordinary" Christian life. That's the context that makes faith beautiful. It also makes life beautiful.

Every Christmas, every year, we're invited to remember.

And give them victory o'er the grave

He is not here. He is risen from the dead, just as he said. Come and see the place where he lay!

—Matthew 28:6

Bilbo finds a ring.

A group of children fall through a wardrobe into another dimension.

Cinderella finds the love of her life. William Wallace loses the love of his.

The old man in the sea hooks a monster fish.

Maximus is named emperor by Marcus Aurelius.

Joseph loves Shannon.

Every story has one truth at its foundation. Without it, there's no story.

There are over 450,000 words stretching from Tolkien's *Silmarillion* to the end of the *Return of the King*. If you stood them on top of each other they'd probably tower over the Empire State Building. But if you remove the words "Bilbo found a ring" from somewhere around the fifth floor, they'd all come tumbling down. Without that, there's no story. Orcs, elves, hobbits, talking trees . . . Who cares?

There is one claim made by one faith.

Without it, the rest of the story of that faith doesn't really matter. All of Jesus' teachings, and his dying, wouldn't matter. Actually, the rest of the story of the universe, and of your life, wouldn't make much sense either.

That one claim was made in a quiet cemetery in an outpost of the Roman Empire. It was carried on the trembling lips of a reformed harlot to a group of terrified fishermen. It was spoken in whispers. A secret too good to be true. Yet it was true. It is true. So true, in fact, that eyewitnesses died horrible deaths attesting to it. (You'll find people who die for belief systems. Dying for an eyewitness testimony is vastly different than that!)

Within three hundred years, this one true claim transformed the Roman Empire.

These three words continue to transform everything they touch, until the story of time is done: "He is risen."

"Cinderella finds love." The one truth is found somewhere in the story, but really, the whole story is found in that one truth.

The whole story of the universe, of human history, of Christianity, and of our own lives are found in these three words: "He is risen!"

This one truth is the proof that God is real. Love wins. And life is good.

And if that's not true . . . who cares about a baby born in an outpost in the Roman Empire, or the rest of the story, or life itself, for that matter?

Part II

LIVING
THE BEST
NEWS EVER.
EVERY DAY.

Faith of our fathers, holy faith, we will be true to thee till death

Lord I believe. Help my unbelief. —Mark 9:24

My mother-in-law, Sylvia, was up late talking to her brother-in-law Ed, trying to convince him about the existence of God. Their conversation stretched into the night. Finally, he stammered, "Well, if God picked up this table in front of me," he said, "then I'd believe in him." A minute later he chuckled, "Actually, I probably still wouldn't believe in him!"

God generally leaves enough wiggle room for us to interpret things the way we choose. This even applies to one of his most dramatic interactions with mankind in history: when he freed his people from slavery in Egypt.

Every plague God unleashed on the Egyptians to force Pharaoh to let his people go also had a natural (though highly unlikely) explanation. It seems that Pharaoh chose to interpret everything that was happening as *really* bad luck. And even after the slaying of the first-born, which he couldn't explain away as a natural phenomenon, his pride still won out. He decided to ignore God and chase down the Hebrews, which ended in the sea swallowing his army . . . which modern day doubters explain away by a change in the tides that day, to which modern day believers would reply, "Tide change or not, it was obviously an act of divine intervention."

Jesus himself said that for those who don't believe, "They won't be persuaded even if someone should rise from the dead" (Luke 16:31). Turns out he was right.

As good as our reasons are for faith, we can't study our way into belief. That's because the endgame isn't a topic; it's a relationship with a person. It's like marriage. A man meets a woman and if she meets enough "checks" on his list, his will eventually has to move beyond where his intellect can go, as he produces a ring and asks the question, "Will you marry me?"

The same is true with faith. I can present good reasons to believe that there is a God and that his name is Jesus. But at the end of the day, reason brings us to the door, but we have to choose to walk through it.

But how?

Want to believe? Act like you believe.

Before entering the waters of holy baptism, people are asked a series of questions to which they choose to respond, "I do." Spend a minute asking yourself these questions, and choosing faith today by saying "I do!" out loud to each one.

Do you believe in God, the Father almighty, creator of heaven and earth?

I do!

Do you believe in Jesus Christ, his only Son, our Lord, who was born of the Virgin Mary, was crucified, died, and was buried, rose from the dead, and is now seated at the right hand of the Father?

I do!

Do you believe in the Holy Spirit, the holy Catholic Church, the communion of saints, the forgiveness of sins, the resurrection of the body, and life everlasting?

I do!

This is our faith. This is the faith of the Church. We are proud to profess it, in Christ Jesus our Lord.

Amen.

Till he appeared and the soul felt its worth

You shall be called by a new name. —Isaiah 62:2

The woman caught in adultery bore the name: whore. Until a man stood between her and her executioners. "Let anyone without sin cast the first stone!" One by one they walked away. "Is there anyone left who condemns you? Neither do I. Go and sin no more."

Peter bore a name: unworthy. He fell to his knees and said, "Depart from me Lord. I'm a sinful man." Jesus saw something more in Peter than he saw in himself. "Come follow me. You'll be a fisher of men."

St. Paul was a persecutor of Christians. In one of the simplest, most heroic acts in early Christian history, Ananias, who had been hiding from Paul, went to pray over him. He didn't say, "Saul, you murderer." He said, "Saul, my brother, our Lord sent me."

Forgiven. Fisher of men. Brother.

What have you named yourself?

Never underestimate the power of the words you use to describe yourself. Words shape our self-perception. Self-perception shapes our actions. Actions shape our lives.

Sometimes our self-labels come from the wrong places. Abuse tells us "you're powerless." Sin tells us "you're dirty." Not being affirmed tells us "you'll never be enough." It's time to get our name from the Word of God!

Christianity doesn't only reveal the truth about who God is. It reveals the truth about who we are.

The truth about *you* is that you have a God and savior who preferred the dwelling of your heart (as messy as it is in there) to a throne in heaven. Who left his glory for a manger where animals ate. For you. A God who thought you were worth dying for. When you hear false identities whispered in your ear, replace them with your real identity: Loved. I don't mean that figuratively. I mean it literally. Say it to others. Look in the mirror and speak the truth to yourself. "I am beautiful." "I am good." "I am redeemed." "I am a daughter/son of God." "I am loved."

God didn't give us his word so we'd wait for "professionals" to preach it to us. Don't wait for me to do that for you. Preach the truth to yourself. Claim your new name and watch your life follow.

Let every heart prepare him room

Repent! —Matthew 3:2

"But when finally the scrolls of history are completed down to the last word of time, the saddest line of all will be: 'There was no room in the inn.'" —Archbishop Fulton J. Sheen

If you want to prepare room in your life for Jesus, some of the things in your life have to be cleared out. That means change. Repentance. Conversion.

I know. Those aren't the most exciting words. Change is scary! But Jesus was excited to call people to repent. I don't think that was as much because of his hatred of sin as it was from his excitement about forgiveness. "For God did not send his Son to condemn the world but to save the world."

We complicate repentance because we complicate forgiveness.

The other day one of my kids was talking back. Badly. It was one of those moments when, as a dad, I was thinking,

"I can't believe my kid is talking to me like that!" (Parents of teens all have those moments!)

As the conversation went from bad to worse, I realized that he was thinking the same thing. "I can't believe I'm saying this." He'd lost control. He was just mad. His own words were starting to hurt him. It happens to the best of us.

I had a grace-filled moment in which I switched from parental rage to compassion. I interrupted him and said, "I forgive you." He kept talking so I said it louder, "I forgive you!" I walked up to him, hugged him, and said a third time, "I forgive you." He choked out a few tears. "I'm sorry, dad."

As I reflected on what happened with my son, I realized that's what Jesus did for us. The cross is God shouting to the world, "I forgive you! I forgive you! I forgive you!"

Saying we're sorry doesn't make forgiveness happen. Saying we're sorry lets us receive the forgiveness that we're already being offered—all the time.

It really is that simple.

Stop pretending your sin isn't sin. You know it is. And it's hurting you.

Stop giving in to that shame that makes you feel the need to cover up every flaw and makes facing your flaws an impossible burden.

Stop holding on to the need to be right all the time.

Let go of the fear of what you'll be like when you give up your favorite sin. As if God wants to deprive you of life?

Try sitting in adoration and letting him love you. When you know how loved you are, it's safe to admit you were wrong. Forgiveness is waiting. And make a habit of it! At the end of every day, examine your conscience and say "I'm sorry" to God, and while you're at it, resolve to say "I'm sorry" to anyone you hurt.

Gloria in excelsis deo!

I give thanks to God every time I think of you.
—Philippians 1:3

During his visit to St. Patrick's Cathedral in New York City, Pope Francis lamented, "We have to ask ourselves, are we (even) capable of counting our blessings?"

We can be given the greatest gifts in the world. If we don't respond with gratitude it doesn't really matter. It won't penetrate.

I think of the wife who puts up with me, a sunny day, the children who run to me when I pull in the driveway: I'm a super lotto winner! But so often I'm too distracted to take it all in. And that has a direct impact on my happiness.

My poor little girl was totally miserable the other day. "My day was horrible," she said as she loaded her backpack into the car after a rough day in the first grade. I Googled images of children in Haiti so I could show her how lucky is she is. After all, "horrible day" is a relative phrase. Her horrible day consisted of "first-world problems" in a clean, safe school. While I didn't want to diminish those problems, I thought it might help give her perspective if I showed her kids who had had a *really* horrible day . . . but all I could find in Google Images for "children from Haiti" were kids with big, *big* smiles.

Of course those images confirmed what I had preached countless times but momentarily forgotten: *real* happiness (let's call it "joy") is 90 percent attitude and 10 percent circumstance. The poorest places on earth lack material goods but are rich in gratitude for everything. Rich in the knowledge of just how much they need God and need one another. Rich in something Jesus called "poverty of spirit." Maybe that's why children from underdeveloped nations tend to smile more than children of privilege.

Gratitude is powerful! It saves us from an unhealthy negativity. (That's why people in Alcoholics Anonymous are told to "count their gratefuls" every day.) It safeguards relationships, because it lets people know that we don't take them for granted. It protects us from pride, because it reminds us that we are not the ultimate source of all our blessings. It might even make us more successful! People like to bless, promote, and support a humble, grateful person. It's just more enjoyable than blessing someone who acts entitled!

Thankfully, it's not hard to unleash the perspective-changing power of gratitude in your life. All it takes is speaking two words as often as possible: THANK YOU.

Thank your spouse who loves you, even when you're not yourself. Thank your teacher for teaching you. Thank the cop who gave you that ticket for keeping you safe. Thank your friend for the unmerited gift of friendship. Thank your parents for dinner. Thank the people in your life who wrapped a present for you. Thank those who are in your life and gave you someone to wrap a present for. And above all, build up your thankful spirit by counting your blessings and thanking God for them every day—starting with the gift of himself out of love for you.

Gratitude might not change your circumstances, but it does change you.

In the words of Venerable Solanus Casey, it's "'heaven begun,' for the grateful on earth."

Lord Jesus, thank you for the gift of my life. Even getting to exist is a gift! I guess everything on top of that is an added bonus! I'm sorry for taking so much for granted. Today I will express my gratitude to those people in my life who I take for granted. And I thank you for [insert five things you're grateful for here]. THANK YOU!

Rest beside the weary road, and hear the angels sing!

Martha, Martha, you are anxious and worried about many things. There is need of only one thing. —Luke 10:41-42

We're all familiar with the Gospel story in which Mary is sitting at Jesus' feet while her sister Martha does the cooking and cleaning. When Martha complains about the obvious, Jesus says, "Martha, Martha, you are anxious and worried about many things. There is need of only one thing. Mary has chosen the better portion."

That Gospel always bothered me! If Martha weren't cooking and cleaning, no one would have eaten!

But if you think about it, Jesus didn't say, "Martha, Martha, stop cooking." He said, "Stop being anxious about many things."

The Christmas season is full of hard work. In fact, sometimes we're so busy we end up snapping at the people we're working hard to create a beautiful Christmas for! But Jesus is telling us "Don't be busy. Be occupied." If there are a hundred things on your plate, make sure only one thing's on your heart.

"There is need of only one thing."

Be present to him in the moment. And all he wants from you in the moment is to be faithful to the task before you with love. You can't do everything at once, so stop attempting the impossible. Take it easy on yourself. Do the one thing, and do it well, listening to him all the while.

Lord, help me to BE like Mary when I have to WORK like Martha.

Now bring him incense, gold, and myrrh

For God so loved the world that he gave his one and only Son. —John 3:16

The gift that God presents to humanity, and that we celebrate every Christmas, is the gift of himself.

We celebrate Christmas year after year by giving "stuff" to each other. But my prayer for you, and for myself this Christmas, is that we don't get so caught up in the "busyness" of the holiday that we forget the most important gift we can offer—ourselves.

I know. You're crazy busy. But pause for just a minute from cooking that Christmas meal and tell your loved ones how much they mean to you. Put aside your work and spend thirty minutes playing that board game with your son. No doubt he'll be happy to unwrap that game under the tree, but your undivided attention will be the far greater gift. As you run around buying presents, try to be present to the people you're buying them for.

And take time to give your heart to God. In addition to Christmas Mass, one simple and beautiful tradition we have as a family is to read about the birth of Jesus from Luke, Chapter 2, before the kids rip into the gifts on Christmas Day.

"Come, let us adore him!" But let's follow his example, too. Don't just share presents and food this Christmas. Share yourself.

Mele Kalikimaka

You are my friends. —John 14:15

Hawaiian islanders have a unique way of greeting one another. They touch foreheads and breathe in deep through their noses. They share breath, a symbol of life itself. Aloha means "with breath."

Sometimes white people are referred to as "haole" in Hawaii. Haole means "without breath." When Hawaiians met the first Europeans, instead of being greeted with a shared breath, the Europeans extended a hand, and shook, thus earning the name.

The intimate greeting of the Hawaiians lends insight into what communion between people is all about. And what we're so often lacking.

We tend to let our acquaintances remain shallow, our work or even church relationships remain corporate, our family lives centered around a million activities. But do we stop to share a breath? Share life? Do we become friends? Do we stop to ask someone how they're really doing, and then really listen?

It doesn't take much time to forge deeper connections. We just have to be intentional about it.

I was lucky enough to film a TV show and do some speaking in Hawaii last summer—and was even luckier that I got to bring my family.

One day while I was walking to the beach to bodysurf, my teenage girl stopped me. "Dad. Sit with me. Let's just talk." We sat on a bench near the beach and talked for an hour. It might have been the best hour of my vacation. And I know she'll never forget just sitting for an hour with her dad's undivided attention. And I didn't even need to cross an ocean to do that!

Those little moments mean the world. Be intentional about grabbing them with the people you love—moments when your attention isn't on much but each other, even if there isn't a lot to say, even if it's for five minutes. Take your kid out for a dollar ice cream cone or sit and sip a glass of wine with your spouse or a good friend. It's important to remember that we only get so many breaths to enjoy those moments together.

Be with me Lord Jesus, I ask thee to stay

In your presence there is fullness of joy. —Psalm 16:11

As Venerable Solanus Casey said, "Man's greatness lies in his capacity to be faithful to the moment." Maybe that's because God, with all his grace and blessings for us, resides in the present moment! But it doesn't take much to drag us out of the present moment.

I could be in the most beautiful place on Earth, but if there's a bug right in front of my face, that's all I'll notice.

Family, community, a hard day's work, good food—all the things you encounter at Christmas—those are the simple things that makes life beautiful! And so often, that's the stuff we don't *really* notice.

How many times have I come home and my little girl runs to me for a hug and I'm not fully present because of something annoying that happened at work? How many times have I've raced through a meal my wife made because of the next thing I have to get to? How many days have kind of passed me by because of plans I'm making for tomorrow? How many moments have I not given my full attention to because half of my brain was occupied by something interesting on my smartphone?

We live in the most distracted era in history. We've all heard the myth that some people are great multitaskers. Not true. I don't care who you are. The more things you do at one time, the more you stink at doing all of them! And the more things you focus on at one time, the less focused you are on each of them. Our brains only have so much bandwidth.

What pulls *you* away from the present moment? On holidays you're pretty good at putting those things aside (and if you're not, turn that smartphone off, or be intentional about getting rid of whatever distracts *you* the most!). But let your holidays be practice for your everyday.

There is a time and a place for everything. A time to work. A time to put distractions aside and rest. You should do that intentionally. Daily.

The moment you're in RIGHT NOW is a gift from God! That's why it's called "the present." Don't let the blessings of today pass you by because of a little bug in front of your eye.

In all our trials, born to be our friend. He knows our need.

Behold, I make all things new. —Revelation 21:5

Life is full of happiness, but it's also full of pain. For many, holidays are also a time when that pain or loss is felt most keenly. Thankfully there's something deeper than "holiday cheer" in the joy of the Gospel. There's hope. That's the story of all the saints.

St. John Paul II lost his mom when he was eight. His big brother when he was twelve. He watched his hometown get taken over by Nazis when he was a teenager, and shortly after by Communists. His dad died when he was twenty. As an old man he reflected, "At twenty I had already lost all the people I loved." Yet "Be not afraid!" was a central theme of his pontificate.

St. Josephine Bakhita was kidnapped as a little girl. Sold into slavery. Branded. Beaten so badly she forgot her birth name. She ended up a freed woman, a Christian, and a religious sister. She summed up her life with the words, "I know that I am definitely loved, and whatever happens I am awaited by love. And so my life is good."

Blessed Chiara Badano was diagnosed with cancer when she was sixteen. Suffered horribly. Never accomplished the dreams she had for herself. And died when she was eighteen in 1990. Chiara spent her time in the hospital cheering up her visitors and walking around counseling depressed patients. Her last words were: "Good-bye. Be happy because I am." Google her. You'll see her radiantly joyful face on her deathbed.

St. Paul's life ended with an inglorious beheading on a hill in Rome. His body fell lifeless to the ground. From the outside, his death looked the same as that of any common criminal, but for Paul, as with all the saints, nothing about it was the same. That's because thirty-four years before Paul's death a man was executed on a hill in Jerusalem.

The God-man didn't just redeem us from sin, he redeemed the entire human experience. We still live. Work. Die. But there's a new light that pierces it all.

When Sam and Frodo approached Mount Doom in *Lord of the Rings*, just when all hope was about to fade, Sam looked up: "There, peeping among the cloud-wrack above a dark tor high up in the mountains, Sam saw a white star twinkle for a while. The beauty of it smote his heart, as he looked up out of the forsaken land, and hope returned to him. For like a shaft, clear and cold, the thought pierced him that in the end the Shadow was only a small and passing thing: there was light and high beauty for ever beyond its reach."

When God entered history, it became his-story. Our lives have entered his-story too. That means your life isn't the story of death, dysfunction, poverty, pain, disease, divorce. Those might be pages. But they're taken up into a bigger story. A love story whose glorious end changes the meaning of every page. That might not take away the pain, but it infuses it with a hope, and even joy, that nothing can touch.

Lord God, I tend to see my life in light of whatever circumstance I find myself in. Divorce, cancer, a failure, dysfunctional relationships, a mean boss, or a bully at school. But those are pages. Not the story. Whatever comes my way today, help me to resist letting my emotions get caught up only in the moment, but also to step back and see the big picture, and to remember that life is good, because you ARE love.

Son of God, love's pure light

This is love. Not that we loved God. But God loved us first. —1 John 4:10

Can you believe that this love story, and this way of life, is for *you*? We think it's hard to love God. The reality is that it's hard to accept all this love.

God is calling you. And so often you answer with your "but . . ."

- "But you don't know my past."
- "But I don't have my faith all figured out."
- "But I *really* like my sin."
- "But I don't want to let myself be wrong!"
- "But I [insert your "but" here]."

His love for you is bigger than your "but"!

St. Augustine understood this.

On his path to conversion he once prayed, "Lord, help me be pure, but not yet!" He went on to become a bishop and one of the most influential saints in the Church's history. His writings remain among the most popular spiritual readings to this day—1,600 years after his death. He is the one who prayed the famous prayer: "You have made us for yourself, and our hearts are restless until they rest in you."

The reason he became such a great saint is that when he was far from saintly he came to God with a spirit of brutal honesty. He didn't let his "but" get in the way. He didn't pretend to be someone he wasn't . . . not that he could have fooled God anyway. He came to God saying, "Lord, I'm a mess. That's okay. I'm *your* mess!"

It's a mystery to me why he loves the mess that I am, but I'm glad that he does. The only reason he offers in Scripture is "I love you. I have called you by name. You are mine." I suppose that as a dad I can relate. That's why I love my children, too. It's not because of what they can accomplish. It's because they're mine. I guess that's enough for God, too. I'll take it.

Lord Jesus, I believe you're calling me to yourself. Right here. Right now. Just as I am. And though you love me too much to let me stay as I am, you take me as I am to-day. Help me to begin following you more deeply, knowing that the journey doesn't depend on my strength or perfection, but on your perfect love for me.

What can I give him, poor as I am? If I were a shepherd, I would bring a lamb; if I were a wise man, I would do my part; yet what I can I give him: give my heart.

Jesus said, "It is finished." With that, he bowed his head and gave up his spirit . . . when they came to Jesus and found that he was already dead, they did not break his legs. Instead, one of the soldiers pierced Jesus' side with a spear, bringing a sudden flow of blood and water.
—John 19:30, 33–34

He was born to die. Born to give everything to you. To me. What does he want in return?

When I asked my wife to marry me, I was offering everything to her.

I knelt before her, and the Blessed Sacrament. I wanted God to be at the heart of our love. I thought I'd be "the man," but I was so overcome by the moment that all I could do was laugh. Thankfully, she said yes.

When a man offers a woman everything, that's exactly what he wants back.

Religion would have been so simple if God had only offered us a few rules, tips for living, rituals to keep, and doctrines to learn, but he threw us a huge curveball. He gave us everything.

That means he's not content with us leaving him at an arm's length. He's not impressed by the fact that we went to Catholic school. It's not enough that we follow a few rules. He wants everything.

I've actually had the conversation multiple times with older men who informed me that they're "squared up" with God because they were altar servers for five-plus years in their childhood! That's the kind of religion the Pharisees had with God. All external acts. No heart and soul.

The same love that rewrote the story of the saints, the love that created space and time, the love you and I were born to find, is here, now, inviting a response from us.

Join me in this prayer written by St. Ignatius of Loyola:

Take, Lord, and receive all my liberty,

my memory, my understanding,

and my entire will,

all I have and possess.

You have given all to me.

To you, Lord, I return it.

Everything is yours; do with it what you will.

Give me only your love and your grace,

that is enough for me.

Yonder peasant, who is he? Where and what his dwelling?

Have the same mindset as Jesus Christ: Who, being in the very nature God, did not consider equality with God something to be grasped at. Rather he made himself a servant, taking on the form of a slave. —Philippians 2:5-6

After a fight with my wife, I was complaining to God, "Why does it always have to be about *her*. Can't it be about *me*? Can't *my* needs come first?"

And God answered me.

I'm not one of those who regularly hears God speak, aside from when I read Scripture, or when he speaks in the ordinary ways, through life's experiences and other people. But this time he spoke to me very directly. Not audibly, but in my heart, yet no less clearly than if it had been in my ears.

He said, "You have every right to make it all about you. You have every right to put your own needs first.

You have every right to be average, to be ordinary. You have every right not to become a saint."

Needless to say, I changed my prayer: "God, give me the grace to make my life about her. To put her needs first."

Ironically, when I pray like that—when I choose to serve—I don't only end up holier, I end up happier!

The days that I wake up and say to myself, "My wife is lacking these five traits of a perfect spouse, I should tell her!" aren't my best days! The days I wake up and ask myself how I can make her the happiest wife on earth, I end up being the happiest husband on earth!

How do we develop the mindset of servants? Like this:

1. Say it. Satan's motto is *"Non serviam,"* which is Latin for "I will not serve." I have a dear friend who starts every day by kissing the floor and saying *"Serviam!"* "I will serve."

2. Think small. We often undervalue small acts of service, but really, life consists of small things. If we accomplish anything great by the world's standards, it's usually the result of a million small things. If there's a cathedral it's because a million bricks were laid, one at a time. But enough of the world's standards. In the

eyes of God, even small acts of kindness, like opening a door for a person at work who bothers you, is important. That's a brick laid for the Kingdom of God! Jesus spent the vast majority of his life working, loving, and serving in ways no one noticed. He was giving us an example.

3. Serve the poor. Jesus made it pretty clear that if we don't do something to care for the poor we can't enter the kingdom (Matt. 25). You don't have to do everything. But everyone can do something, from donating online, to giving out food cards to a person on a street corner (no cash please!), to volunteering at a local charity, or all of the above!

Lord Jesus, you call me to turn outside of myself. To be a servant today. That doesn't mean you want me to stuff all my emotional needs, but you want me to be free from my "neediness." You invite me to be other-centered instead of self-centered. Give me the grace to be like you, so I can know the freedom and joy of the saints.

Go, tell it on the mountain!

Go therefore and make disciples of all nations, baptizing them in the name of the Father and of the Son and of the Holy Spirit. —Matthew 28:19

Florence was lying on her deathbed. She'd been a faithful wife, devoted mother, and finally, a loving grandmother to my wife. And for some reason that tortured her conscience in secret, she had confided in my wife years ago that she thought she was going to hell.

Her son, my father-in-law, is a good man, but an agnostic.

So there I was at her deathbed. It's not one of those times you want to rock the boat. That voice in my head told me, "Let her die in 'peace' and quiet. Don't challenge her faith right now! Don't risk conflict with your father-in-law. Don't risk upsetting her." But I knew I had to ignore that voice.

I leaned in close and said, "Jesus was crucified with two thieves. One rejected him. The other said 'Jesus, remember me when you come into your kingdom.' He hadn't done much good throughout his life. But that's all it took for Jesus to say, 'This day you will be with me in paradise.' Florence, that can be you. You just have to receive the mercy of Jesus." The following day she was received into the Catholic Church, and the day after that she went home to our Lord.

What if I hadn't said the uncomfortable? What if her Catholic grandkids and daughter-in-law hadn't prayed by her bedside, and more importantly, shown her the love of Jesus for so many years? What if that priest hadn't decided to drop into the room of a non-Catholic the day after I shared the story of the good thief?

In some mysterious way, God has made the eternal destiny of others contingent on our response to his call to be witnesses, each in our own way.

We presume that the world will be offended whenever we share the love of God. And sometimes people are. But more often than not, we project our discomfort on others, who wouldn't mind us sharing about our faith any more than they'd mind us sharing about our favorite football team.

And if they knew the depth of our faith, frankly, they might be offended if we didn't share it! The famous comedian and atheist Penn Jillette, reflecting on his respect for Christians who have tried to convert him, said, "How much do you have to hate somebody to not evangelize? How much do you have to hate somebody to believe that everlasting life is possible and not tell them that?"

There's an overused saying that we should preach the Gospel at all times and when necessary, use words. Words are often necessary. Use them.

Don't get me wrong, there are times when it's best not to speak. If we overtalk we might scare some people away. But there are also times in our lives when we're called upon to speak up. And you don't have to be a "professional evangelist" to do that.

The whole world tells us to be ourselves, though the world seems to have forgotten what that means! And somehow we've gotten shy about the best news in history!? Friends, sharing the Gospel is as simple as being holy, and then just being yourself. That might be as deep as a deathbed conversation. It might be as simple as a "God bless you" at the checkout counter, "I'm praying for you" to the person who just told you they had a bad day, or "Hey, I haven't seen you in a while. Wanna come to a talk at my parish with me?" If you do that lovingly, I promise that those little witnessing moments will help people think of God even if they pretend to give you a cold shoulder.

The "secret sauce" of salvation history isn't in the big events in the Bible. It's in the most boring chapters: the genealogies. Most of them consist of names we've never heard before. It's not until the end of the long list "and Joseph was the father of Jesus" that we say, "I know those names!" But make no mistake, if it weren't for that long, seemingly insignificant list of names sharing the faith, living good lives—often at great personal sacrifice—and passing on this way of life to the next generation, Joseph would never have had the grit, virtue, and formation he had to do his part for the salvation of the world.

You have no idea how important you are, Christian.

God has entrusted the best news ever to you. Through your words and your actions he's counting on you to share it with the world!

"God bless us, everyone."

Isn't it time to START LIVING
the life you were made for?

God didn't create you just to get by,
he created you to live life to the full!

REDISCOVER GOD AND REDISCOVER THE LIFE
YOU WERE MADE FOR.

A life changing event.

To attend a REBOOT! LIVE! event

with **Chris Stefanick**, or if you're interested in hosting one

at your parish, please visit RealLifeCatholic.com

ABOUT THE AUTHOR

Chris Stefanick is an internationally acclaimed author and speaker, who has devoted his life to inspiring people to live a bold, contagious faith.

Chris's live events reach more than 85,000 people per year. His videos and radio spots and TV show reach more than a million people per month, every month. And his educational initiatives are turning the tide in the Church. He authored what is being welcomed as the best Confirmation program in the English language: Chosen. He also offers several other books, CDs and DVDs.

Chris is also the founder of Real Life Catholic, a Denver-based nonprofit which operates as the head-quarters for Chris's various initiatives.

Above all, Chris is proud to be the husband to his wife Natalie and father to their six children.

To learn more about Chris's work, please visit: www.RealLifeCatholic.com

REAL LIFE CATHOLIC
OUR MISSION

To ignite a bold, contagious faith in the heart of every Catholic in North America.

OUR WORK

We serve Christ and his Church by building a movement of Catholics who share the beauty, power and truth of the Gospel with a world that has largely forgotten. We remind people of the best news in history through a convergence of life-changing LIVE EVENTS; MEDIA, including television, radio, online videos, books and CDs; and, various EDUCATIONAL INITIATIVES, all designed to continually nudge people toward a deeper relationship with Jesus Christ, and a greater confidence for sharing him with the world.

 **RealLifeCatholic.com**

Real Life Catholic
www.RealLifeCatholic.com
Email: info@RealLifeCatholic.com